A
MEDIEVAL
CATHEDRAL

Series Editor	David Salariya
Book Editor	Vicki Power
Design Assistant	Carol Attwood
Consultant	John Gillingham

Author:

Fiona Macdonald studied history at Cambridge University and at the University of East Anglia. She has taught children, adults and undergraduates. She has written many books on historical topics, mainly for children.

Illustrator:

John James was born in London in 1959. He studied at Eastbourne College of Art and has specialized in historical reconstruction since leaving art school in 1982.

Consultant:

John Gillingham studied history at Oxford and Munich universities. Since 1966 he has taught history at the London School of Economics and Political Science. He is the author of books on Richard the Lionheart, the Angevine Empire and the Wars of the Roses. He has also written and presented a TV program on the Magna Carta.

Published by
Peter Bedrick Books
2112 Broadway
New York, NY 10023

Library of Congress Cataloging-in-Publication Data
Macdonald, Fiona.
  A medieval cathedral / Fiona Macdonald : [illustrated by] John
James – 1st American edition.
  (Inside story)
  Includes index.
  Summary: Text and cutaway illustrations depict the construction of a
medieval cathedral and the way of life inside it.
  ISBN 0-87226-350-9
  ISBN 0-87226-266-9 (pbk)
  1. Cathedrals – Juvenile literature. 2. Middle Ages – Juvenile literature. [1.
Cathedrals. 2. Civilization, Medieval.]
I. James, John, 1959 - ill. II. Title. III. Series: Inside story
(Peter Bedrick Books)
NA4830.M34 1991
726'.6'0940902 – dc20   91-16415

Printed in Hong Kong by Wing King Tong Ltd.
94 95 5 4 3

INSIDE ⋀ STORY

A MEDIEVAL CATHEDRAL

FIONA MACDONALD

JOHN JAMES

PETER BEDRICK BOOKS

NEW YORK

Contents

INTRODUCTION

Throughout Europe, we can still see many beautiful medieval cathedrals towering above the roofs of all but the tallest modern skyscrapers. These 'prayers in stone' have survived for centuries, and can still astonish us with their size and grandeur. Today, we admire their beauty, and marvel at the skills of the masons and carpenters who built them. We study them for what they have to tell us about the past, and worry about how to preserve them from decay and pollution. And we respect them as holy places, where people offer prayers and praises to God. The cathedrals shown in this book were mostly built during the Middle Ages (from around 550 to 1450). This was the great age of cathedral-building in Europe. Of course, building did not stop at the end of the medieval period; magnificent new cathedrals are still being constructed today. Now, as then, cathedrals display the might and majesty of the Church; like them, its power and glory seemed certain to endure forever.

CHOOSING THE SITE

In the Middle Ages, as today, the world was divided into regions (called 'sees' or 'dioceses') for the purposes of Church government and administration. Each diocese was ruled by a bishop – a senior clergyman. Medieval bishops usually came from noble or wealthy families. Many of them were well-educated, capable and energetic, and some played a leading part in running the countries in which their dioceses were situated. Not all bishops were conscientious about performing their religious duties. Some used their authority to help them fulfil personal ambitions for wealth and power.

A cathedral is the place where a bishop has his headquarters. The Church's power is symbolized by the bishop's throne, a magnificent raised seat in the holiest part of the cathedral where the bishop sits during services. Medieval bishops chose to build their cathedrals in important towns or cities in their dioceses. Often, a cathedral was built on the site of an earlier church, particularly if it contained holy relics or had been founded by a saint.

The money to build cathedrals came mostly from gifts – of land, farms, houses and jewels, and gold and silver coins. People believed that by giving to the Church, they would help to win forgiveness for their sins.

Bishops sought gifts of land and money from wealthy kings, princes and nobles to help pay for their cathedrals.

Cathedrals were very expensive to build and maintain. They needed frequent repairs, especially to the roof.

Many cathedrals were built on the site of earlier churches, but, since they were larger, they took up a great deal more space. Over the years, bishops added splendid new buildings to their cathedrals to house the clergy who worshipped there. Sometimes houses and shops had to be pulled down to make room; this could lead to trouble between the bishop and the townspeople.

Stages in the development of cathedrals: Roman hall, 2nd century.

Early oratory (place of prayer), built of wood with simple doorway and windows, 627.

Stone-built church with round-arched doors and windows, from the 7th century.

Larger stone church with rounded apse and porch to protect door, Viking period, *c.* 780.

Clearing the site for a new cathedral (below).

Bishop's throne, or cathedra, built in Canterbury Cathedral around 1200, to replace an older one.

J·E·J· MCMXCI

CATHEDRAL ARCHITECTURE

Cathedrals were founded throughout Europe in the Middle Ages, and, in later centuries, have been built all over the world following the spread of the Christian religion. All cathedrals, wherever they are, have the same religious function, which has not changed over the years. As one 5th century writer put it: 'Let there be a throne towards the east, and places for priests to the right and left... the altar ought also to be there....'

Key elements – the bishop's throne, places for clergy (later known as the 'choir') and an altar, where the bishop and priests could celebrate Mass – were found in all cathedrals. In time, extra elements – a nave, where ordinary people stood, chapels to house the relics of saints or an altar dedicated to the Virgin Mary, and towers and spires where bells were hung – were added to cathedrals to meet the needs of the priests and people who worshipped there. Monasteries were attached to many European cathedrals, and the bishop's palace was built nearby.

Medieval cathedrals were built in a wide variety of architectural styles, according to the inventiveness of the cathedral's architect, the fashion of the time, and the tastes of the people who paid for them. This book contains many different examples of cathedral architecture.

Key

1. Aisle Sideways extension of the nave. ('Aisle' literally means 'wing'.)

2. Arcade Row of arches supported by pillars.

3. Buttress A prop made of stone to stop the walls collapsing outwards under the weight of the roof.

4. Bell tower Tower where bells were hung, almost always at the west end of the cathedral. Bells were rung to call worshippers to services at the cathedral.

5. Clerestory A row of windows designed to let extra light into the church or cathedral.

6. Choir The most holy end of the cathedral, nearest to the altar. Cathedral clergy stood in the choir during services.

7. Flying buttress Narrow, graceful buttress shaped like an arch.

8. Foundation A strong platform several yards below ground.

9. Nave The 'body' of the cathedral, where worshippers stood or knelt during services.

10. Porch Provided shelter for worshippers and clergy.

11. Roof Made of lead or sometimes slates or tiles, resting on a framework of wooden rafters.

12. Rose window Large, circular window filled with brilliantly patterned glass. Rose windows symbolized eternity.

13. Spire Tall, pointed structure built on top of one or more towers. Spires were built of wood, and covered with sheets of lead or wooden tiles, known as shingles. Spires were often topped by a golden weather vane or a cross.

14. Transept Extension to the cathedral, usually located where the nave joins the choir. Transepts housed robing rooms for clergy and chapels dedicated to saints.

15. Vault The arched underside of the roof; the area worshippers inside the building saw when they looked upwards.

QUARRYING THE STONE

The earliest Christian churches had been built of wood, or whatever was the cheapest and most readily available building material locally. But gradually, the Church grew more powerful and wealthy. More and more people began to follow its teachings – or as many of them as they felt able. Bishops and priests began to build new and more magnificent churches and cathedrals. To do this, they chose the finest, most long-lasting materials available. Whenever possible, they chose to build their new cathedrals in stone.

Stone was hacked from the face of the quarry by hand, and hauled laboriously to the surface, using cranes or pulleys powered by men and animals. Quarrying was an exhausting, dangerous job. Quarry workers fell ill with diseases caused by dust and damp, and were often horribly injured in rock-falls and landslips. Despite the dangers of the job, they were very poorly paid.

The best building stone in Europe came from France. It was very expensive, largely because of the cost of transportation from the

Masons' tools (left to right): picks and axes for quarrying and shaping stone; hammer and chisel for dressing stone; saw for cutting stone; masons' bucket with lugs (handles) for lifting.

Rock face

Picks

quarry to the building site. In 1287, the builders of Norwich Cathedral ordered a load of stone from Caen, about 300 miles away in northern France. The cost of loading and transporting the stone were nearly twice as much as the stone itself.

Many quarries had a blacksmith's forge (below, far left) and workshop on site, to make, mend and sharpen the iron tools used to cut the stone.

Masons worked in lodges (simple huts) which provided shelter from rain, wind and sun, and served as a place for relaxing and meeting with co-workers.

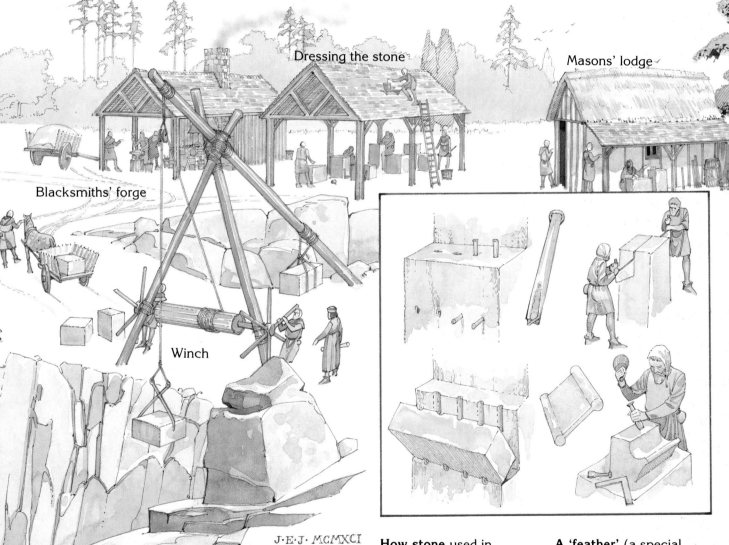

Dressing the stone

Masons' lodge

Blacksmiths' forge

Winch

J·E·J· MCMXCI

Quarries were dangerous places. Workmen climbed down to the workface by means of wooden scaffolding and ladders. Floods and landslips often caused accidents.

How stone used in building the cathedrals was cut (above). First, blocks were rough-sawn into shape – hard and exhausting work. Then the mason made a row of holes in the surface of the block, using a star-chisel and a mallet (a heavy hammer).

A 'feather' (a special metal tool, illustrated above) was then hammered into the stone, along the row of holes. This split the stone neatly and precisely. Finally, the stone was shaped by the carver with a fine chisel and a lighter mallet.

FOUNDATIONS

The second most important building material used in medieval cathedrals was wood. Oak was the best timber – it was beautiful to look at, hard, strong, and lasted for centuries. Like good quality stone, it was expensive to buy, and even more expensive to transport. Whenever possible, it was carried by water, since this was the easiest and cheapest method of moving heavy loads in medieval times. Otherwise, wood was loaded on to carts pulled by horses or oxen, and hauled along bumpy roads to the nearest port.

Lighter, less durable wood like pine or ash was used to make scaffolding, ladders and all kinds of lifting machinery used in building the great cathedrals. And, of course, the ships and carts used to carry the stone and timber were themselves made out of wood.

While the wood and stone were being chosen and transported, workers at the cathedral site were busy laying out the foundations. It might take hundreds of years to complete a cathedral, but the overall shape was often planned right from the start.

Marking out the foundations for a new cathedral building with rope and wooden pegs, later used as a guide by the workmen digging the foundation trenches.

Medieval surveyors did not have modern instruments to help them. To make straight lines and square corners, they measured using a right-angled triangle.

Limestone was the most popular medieval building stone because it was easy to work.

Plan of a typical medieval cathedral (right), showing walls and windows, and also the position of the pillars supporting the roof. There is a large porch, known as a 'galilee', at the west end, and a semicircular space, known as an 'apse', at the east end. The nave was where ordinary people stood or knelt to hear services, while the cathedral clergy stood in a place called the choir. There were extra chapels (places for prayer) in the transepts, and a central tower built above the space where the nave joined the choir. Deep foundations had to be dug beneath the building by workmen to help support the huge weight of the cathedral.

Thousands of trees were needed to build a cathedral. Oak was the best and strongest wood, but by the 12th century it was already becoming scarce and expensive, and in France people complained about the great oak forests being cut down for building.

Underground chapels called crypts (right) were sometimes built beneath new cathedrals as final resting places for the bodies of saints. Many of these crypts can still be seen in medieval cathedrals.

Aisle · Nave · Galilee · Transept · Chapel · Central tower · Choir · Apse

J·E·J· MCMXCI

CRAFTSMEN

Master stone cutter

Stone dresser

The architect and master mason planned and supervised the building work.

Master mason

Architect

Laborers

Laborers carried the stones from wagons and barges to the site.

The master stone cutter chose the best blocks of stone for each purpose.

The stone dresser cut the stone into rough shape for the sculptors.

Medieval cathedrals, constructed hundreds of years ago, are still among the largest buildings in the world. With a few exceptions, their walls, towers and foundations have remained strong for centuries, and the beauty and magnificence of their structures – as well as the inventiveness of their design – still have the power to astonish and delight.

The men responsible for planning the layout and construction of cathedrals were known as architect-engineers. (In the Middle Ages, there was no opportunity for women to study architecture, or to work on building sites.) These architects were highly skilled and, once they had made a name for themselves, in great demand all over Europe.

Stone carvers

The stone carvers shaped stone into graceful and elaborate patterns for use in window frames, doorways and arches.

Carpenters made strong scaffolding to support windows and arches while they were being built. Most cathedral roofs were wooden, with massive oak timbers for tie beams and rafters.

Carpenters

Sculptors carved statues showing saints and Biblical characters to decorate the cathedral.

Sculptors

Mortar makers

Stones were held together with mortar, a mixture of sand, quicklime and water, mixed together using wooden spades.

For example, in 1129 the architect Raymond agreed his fees with the archbishop. Each year he was to be paid six silver coins, thirty-six lengths of cloth, seventeen loads of wood, as many shoes and gaiters as he required, plus a measure of salt and a pound of wax for candles – an expensive luxury.

Craftsmen, who worked as masons, carvers, carpenters, blacksmiths, roofers and glaziers, were also paid well for their work. In early 14th century England, master masons earned about double the salary an ordinary farm worker might get. They were helped on site by laborers and rough workmen, and by apprentices practicing their skills.

Blacksmiths repaired and sharpened building tools and also made decorative ironwork.

Blacksmith

Roofer

Glass blowers produced hand made glass for cathedral windows.

Stained glass craftsmen designed windows in colored glass.

Glass maker

Stained glass craftsmen

Plumbers coated cathedral roofs with sheets of lead to provide a waterproof covering.

J·E·J·MCMXCI

STONE TRACERY

Once the foundations of the cathedral were laid down, the architect and the master masons had to design and build the walls and windows. Walls, pillars and windows had a double function to perform. They had to be strong and sturdy enough to support the roof of the cathedral, but they also had to be beautiful to look at. The architect worked out his designs, probably sketching them on parchment, and perhaps copying some features from other buildings he had seen. Then he traced them out on the floor of a large covered space, where the masons could use them as life-size patterns to follow when carving their finished stonework.

For many of the most intricate sections of stonework, the masons first made wooden templates, or models, to guide them. These could be pieced together, trimmed and adjusted to ensure an exact fit. The most skilled workmen carried out all the elaborate and delicate stone carving, leaving the simpler sections of windows and arches to

Designs for window tracery (top). Arches and carved pillars were copied from the architect's sketches by scratching the outlines into a thin layer of plaster spread on the tracing room floor.

Architects and masons in medieval times were sometimes forced to make life-sized, three dimensional models of parts of the cathedral. This is because they had no mathematical skills like geometry or trigonometry that help today's architects draw up small scale plans for builders to work from.

Architects checked the finished carvings against their plans (left). Remains of the tracing floor at York Minster, England, have survived, complete with the architect's designs.

Architects and master masons were treated like gentlemen and received at the courts of kings. They wrote and received letters, owned manors and quarries and were buried in fine tombs.

be completed by apprentices or less able workers. When the work was finished, the separate pieces of stone were hauled into position and securely fixed together with a layer of mortar – a mixture of water, sand and quicklime, which set hard to form a permanent bond.

Complicated, finely detailed stone carvings (right), like this doorway decorated with saints and angels, were also planned and laid out in the tracing room. Master craftsmen and sculptors then worked on separate parts of the design before the whole was assembled and moved into position.

J·E·J· MCMXCI

THE WORKER'S DAY

6 am (still dark) Gets up, washes hands and face, gets dressed.

6.30 am Breakfast with family: bread, cheese, skim milk, ale or cider.

7 am (sunrise) Off to work at the cathedral building site in town.

7.30 am Takes orders from master carpenter; is sent to fetch wood.

9 am Returns from timber yard with piece of oak for carving.

10 am Dinner: meat pie, pancakes, ale, fetched from cooks' stalls.

10.30 am Back to work; starts to shape wood for door frame.

2 pm Called over to help move finished choir stalls into cathedral.

They have been carved in the lodges on site and are ready to be moved.

4 pm Stalls in place; carpenters thanked by man who paid for them.

6 pm (dusk) Time to go home; packs up tools and locks them in lodge.

6.30 pm Back home for supper: dried pea soup, bread, ale. Hears gossip and news from family.

7.30 pm Commotion outside; a robbery from a house nearby. Cloth and pewter dishes taken. All

rush out to try to catch the thieves, but they escape and disappear down a dark alleyway.

9.30 pm Neighbor calls; reports that night watchman has caught the thieves redhanded.

Above them came apprentices, boys being trained in one of the different crafts. Apprentices lived in the houses of master craftsmen and helped them in their work in return for being taught their trade. When an apprenticeship was over, they would become journeymen, paid by the day or by piecework for careful, responsible work. Only the best journeymen would become master craftsmen, whose work was widely admired.

Building a medieval cathedral might take hundreds of years, and so whole colonies of workmen settled in the towns where cathedrals were being built. They knew that there would always be work for them, and perhaps for their children and grandchildren, too. Medieval craftsmen worked from sunrise to sunset; this meant that their working day was longer in the summer. But they had many more holidays, to celebrate religious festivals, saints' days and traditional feasts, than most modern workers.

Not all craftsmen were hard-working. Often, the overseers on building sites complained about slackness and absenteeism. Many different kinds of workmen were involved in building a cathedral. At the lowest grade, there were untrained laborers, who did all the dirty, heavy jobs that required muscle power.

J·E·J· MCMXCI

The carpenter's wife is also busy all day. She cooks, cleans, shops, washes and mends clothes, and spins fine linen thread to sell.

BUILDING THE WALLS

Cathedral walls and pillars were massive structures, often enclosing hundreds of square yards. Although they were built of stone, they were not quite as solid as they looked. Usually, walls and pillars were constructed of two separate layers, an outer casing of neatly squared stone blocks, known as ashlar, carefully fitted together, and an inner core, or filling, of rough stone, rubble and mortar. Journeymen and laborers prepared the core, while skilled master masons chiselled the ashlar facing blocks. They often 'signed' these by carving their own 'mason's mark' into the finished stone.

Designs and decorations used in cathedral building changed quite considerably over the centuries, although the basic plan of most cathedrals remained the same. The earliest surviving cathedrals, dating from the 10th to the 12th centuries, are built in a style known as 'Romanesque', with squat, solid pillars and heavy rounded arches. The elaborate doorway at the bottom of page 17 is in Romanesque style. Later medieval cathedrals dating from the 13th to the 15th centuries are built in a lighter style, usually known as Gothic. They have pointed arches, slender columns and soaring roofs, like the elegant section of Chartres Cathedral in France, shown in the picture on this page.

A scene portrayed in a 13th century stained glass window (far right) shows master masons at work. The man on the right of the picture is wearing a glove to protect his chisel-holding hand. The masons' templates (shapes used to help them cut complicated patterns) and compasses hang overhead. Their set squares (used to measure right angles) lie on the ground.

A 13th century manuscript drawing showing masons and other craftsmen at work (top inset). The man on the left of the picture is using a level with an adjustable plumbline; below him, a man is hauling up a basket of stones with a windlass. In the center of the picture, a mason is checking the level of a newly positioned block of stone with a weighted line – there is a bowl filled with mortar by his feet – while below him, a skilled craftsman carves decorations for the top of a pillar. At the far right of the picture, a scaffolder perched halfway up a ladder bores a hole in a wooden post; below him, a carpenter shapes a beam with an axe.

Scaffolding, invented during medieval times, was so important to the building work that it was designed at the same time as the cathedral.

J·R·J· MCMXCI

DRAINS, GARGOYLES AND ROOFS

Once each section of the cathedral walls was completed, it had to be roofed over and made weatherproof. The earliest cathedral roofs were made of timber, but, whenever possible, these were replaced with stone, to lessen the risk of fire. But stone roofs were expensive, extremely heavy and took a long time to build. Cathedral walls began to bulge outwards under the extra weight, and often had to be supported by rows of stone buttresses. Building these involved extra expense in materials and workmanship.

Nonetheless, the risk of fire – from stray sparks from nearby houses, from unattended candles, or occasionally from lightning – was so great that stone roofs were still preferred, despite the problems they brought. Medieval architects were also worried by the difficulties of carrying up the large quantities of water needed to put out fires. For this reason, they designed special stairs and passageways within the great cathedral walls to allow fire fighters quick and easy access to the roof. Whatever they were made of, cathedral roofs still had to be covered with something to keep out the rain. Thin sheets of lead, which could be welded together to make a completely waterproof 'skin', were the first choice, but lead was expensive. Sometimes clay tiles or slates were used instead.

Drains were essential to carry rain water down from the high cathedral roof. Often, they were hidden in buttresses or pinnacles. Gargoyles (far right) were used as water spouts, to carry streams of rain water away from the walls. Masons usually carved them like monsters or devils. But sometimes they made mocking portraits of bishops or craftsmen instead.

Long strips of lead, known as flashing, were used to cover gaps between roofs and walls. The edge of the flashing was curved back to stop water seeping in.

Plumbers at work (below, far right inset): First, sheets of lead were prepared from 'pigs' (solid blocks of lead). The pig was heated until it melted and then the molten lead was poured into a level bed lined with sand. It was then left to cool. The finished sheets of lead were about one yard wide and several yards long. Though heavy, they were flexible and quite easy to work, and could be joined to form large sheets to cover a roof, or rolled around wooden posts to create drainpipes and gutters.

The slope of a lead roof could not be very steep, because lead was so heavy it would tear away and roll down the roof like a carpet.

J·E·J·MCMXCI

Lead casters

Rolling lead sheets

FLOORS AND VAULTS

Even when the roof of a medieval cathedral was safely in place, the masons and stone carvers still had to decorate the ceiling, which worshippers could look up at and admire. The craftsmen also had to find a strong covering for the cathedral floor.

The earliest cathedral roofs were simple wooden rafters covered with slates or tiles. As building techniques developed, 'barrel vaults' were used. They were like the inside of a tunnel, with a row of semicircular arches supporting a smooth, curved surface in between. Roofs like this could be boarded over, or covered with plaster to form a plain ceiling. Later architects were more ambitious, and designed roofs with soaring, arched stone vaults. The stone arches formed a complicated pattern of criss-cross 'ribs' stretching diagonally across the space between the pillars. (The four drawings at the bottom of these pages show how this worked.) Over the years, ribs were arranged in ever more elaborate patterns. Eventually, most 'rib-vaulting' served no structural purpose at all, but was purely for decoration.

Designs for mazes (above) from five medieval cathedrals.

Designs for windows (below), from 11th to 14th centuries.

Cathedral floors (below) were decorated with patterned tiles, made of fired (baked) clay with designs in colored and pigmented glazes.

Stages in building a rib-vaulted roof are shown above. First, a wooden framework (called centering) was made and put into position.

Then stone arches (or ribs) were built above the centering, criss-crossing the space above the pillars and forming a strong,

J·E·J· MCMXCI

Laying the great maze (above), to form part of the cathedral floor. The stones and tiles were laid on a level base of sand, and held in place by mortar.

1. Romanesque arch.
2. Gothic arch.

Right: Roof bosses were used to decorate vaulted roofs. These examples come from Norwich Cathedral in England.

Cathedral floors were covered with stone slabs, decorated clay tiles and, sometimes mazes made of different colored marble. Not many mazes survive, but Chartres Cathedral in France has a fine one that is 52 feet in diameter.

lightweight 'cage'. The space in between the stone ribs could then be filled in with even lighter materials, such as bricks and plaster. These formed the inner roof covering. Finally, the wooden centering was taken away. Sometimes the bricks and plaster were decorated.

'THE BIBLE OF THE POOR'

Towards the end of the 15th century, the French poet François Villon wrote the following lines describing how his elderly mother, a poor peasant woman, might feel when she walked into her beautifully decorated local village church:

'I am a woman, poor and old,
Quite ignorant, I cannot read.
They showed me, in my village church
A painted Paradise with harps
And Hell where the damned souls are boiled.
One gives me joy, the other frightens me....'

Until the later Middle Ages, most ordinary people could not read or understand the words of church services, which were in Latin. The only ways they had of learning about Christianity were by listening to sermons or by looking at the scenes from saints' lives and Bible stories shown in wall paintings, statues and stained glass.

The brilliantly colored glass used in medieval cathedrals was made in special workshops established in major towns. Chemicals were mixed with the molten glass to produce glowing colors, and the designs were pieced together and held secure by thin strips of lead. In the 14th century, craftsmen discovered a way of painting on glass using a special silver stain, to add greater richness and detail to their designs.

Installing a great 'rose window'. These dramatic circular windows were first introduced during the 12th century in France, and became very popular. The circular design was thought to represent the petals of a flower opening towards the sun. Rose windows gave craftsmen the chance to show their skill, and still survive at Chartres Cathedral in France, and York Minster in England.

Stained glass windows took skilled craftsmen many hours to build. First, glass was made by melting sand, lime and potash together. The glass blower then blew the molten glass into a cylindrical shape, which was cut open and flattened. The glass worker cut the glass roughly according to the window design by touching it with a hot iron and pouring cold water over the heated areas, causing the glass to break along the 'hot spots'. Workers then used a tool called a 'grozing iron' to cut the glass into smaller pieces. The glass was then painted with a special paint which, when heated, melted into the glass. The glass pieces were fitted together with lengths of lead called 'cames', and the joints fixed with drops of molten solder, a mixture of lead and tin.

Bell towers and spires

Cathedrals were built to be noticed. First of all, they were designed to give honor and glory to God, but they also brought fame and a measure of fortune to the men who designed and built them, and to the towns where they stood. One of the best ways of making a huge cathedral even more noticeable was by adding to its height by building a tower or a spire. These tall 'fingers' also pointed to heaven, and so served as a constant reminder of God to all.

Towers also had a useful purpose, for housing clocks and bells. Peals of bells were rung to summon worshippers to services in churches and cathedrals. In the early Middle Ages clocks were unknown, and so time was measured by specially marked candles (which burned a known number of inches per hour) or, more usually, by hourglasses (filled with sand) and sundials fixed on outside walls. But by the 13th century, medieval scientists and engineers began to design mechanical devices to tell the time. The earliest surviving European clock, as we would recognize it today, is thought to be the one at Salisbury Cathedral in England. Bells and clocks were given to cathedrals in the hope of winning God's pardon for sins, or in memory of well-loved or famous people who had died.

Bishops and townspeople competed to build the largest and most beautiful cathedral. The tallest medieval cathedral spire was at Strasbourg in France. Almost 490 feet high (as high as a 45-story building today), it remained the tallest building in Europe for hundreds of years, until the Eiffel Tower was built in Paris during the 19th century using newly invented cast iron.

Bells were cast in molds (right). First, a life-size model of the bell was made from clay. It was coated with a layer of wax and covered with more clay, leaving a few channels leading to the outside. The whole block was heated, and the liquid wax trickled away. Melted bell-metal was then poured into the mold to replace the wax. It was left to harden, and then the clay mold was broken.

Spires were usually made of wood, covered with thin sheets of lead, which made them very heavy. They were also fragile and liable to be blown down in high winds. And, because they were covered with metal, they were often struck by lightning. Many cathedrals were damaged when their tall spires and heavy bell towers crashed to the ground, smashing through the roof and damaging the nave.

J·F·J· MCMXCI

VISIONS OF HEAVEN

Medieval churches and cathedrals were decorated with wall paintings, carvings, statues and other precious objects to add to their beauty and splendor. However, as Abbot Suger, head of the the French abbey of St Denis, wrote in the early 12th century, displaying these treasures had another purpose: to 'show simple people...what they must believe'. Churches and cathedrals, glittering with gold and jewels, glowing with light and color, and headily perfumed with incense, must often have seemed to 'simple people' like a foretaste of heaven, at least as medieval preachers described it.

Among the most sumptuous of medieval cathedral treasures were richly embroidered robes, altar cloths, banners and wall hangings. Craftworkers, monks and nuns produced many outstanding embroideries. English church embroidery was especially famous. When the Normans invaded England in 1066, one of William the Conqueror's barons reported that 'the women of England are very skilful with the needle.' He praised the elaborate cloths worked with silk and gold that were exported throughout Europe. When Thomas Selmiston, an English monk, died in 1419, he was mourned because 'he was in the art of embroidery a most cunning artificer, having none like him.'

Split stitch (above left), one of the most commonly used stitches in medieval embroidery.

Vestments (robes) worn by bishops and priests (above) were often embroidered by women.

Tapestries and embroidered hangings (above) were stretched on a frame to support the weight of the fabric while it was worked.

Artists made their own paints (above and right), using pestles and mortars for mixing and grinding. Color came from powdered pigments – minerals such as lapis lazuli (a beautiful blue) or red lead. To make paint, they were mixed with a sticky, liquid medium which sometimes contained egg yolks or 'size' made from boiled animal hoofs and horns. Thin sheets of pure gold, known as gold leaf, were also glued to paintings to add richness and luster.

Alabaster tomb effigy (life-size statue) of Alice de la Pole, Duchess of Suffolk, who died in 1475.

Elaborately decorated tomb (right), carved around 1330, of Marie de Valois, Queen of Naples in Italy.

PRIESTS AND PEOPLE

Since cathedrals were so large, and took so long to build, many bishops must have spent the whole of their period in office – perhaps twenty years or more – attempting to hold services or run their dioceses in the middle of a vast building site. What were a medieval bishop's responsibilities towards the people – and buildings – in his care?

One writer of the Middle Ages described the duties of a bishop like this: '...his prayers first, then his book-work, reading or writing, teaching or learning; and then his church hours [services] at the right time;...and his alms-giving; and the supervision of work... and, at public meetings, he ought often and frequently to teach knowledge of the Christian faith among the people....'

Throughout the Middle Ages, bishops' spiritual duties remained much the same, and they are still very similar today. Many bishops also played an active part in politics, acting as government ministers and advisors to kings and princes. In medieval England, bishops were summoned to Parliament, where they sat in the House of Lords. Bishops were also responsible for all the priests, monks and nuns in their dioceses, and for administering the large estates that had been given by wealthy and religious people to help build and maintain their cathedrals.

1. **A candlestick** of enormous proportions, from St. Remi at Rheims in France.
2. **A box made of gold** and jewels containing the relics of a saint.
3. **Gold container** shaped like a dove.
4. **Gilt and bronze** lectern (reading stand).
5. **Ivory carving** showing Jesus on the cross.
6. **Top part** of bishop's crozier (staff), made of gold and silver.
7. **A model rose**, made of gold, silver and jewels, from the cathedral in Basel, Switzerland.
8. **A cross**, carried in processions, made of silver and decorated with exquisite enamel-work.
9. **Female artist** painting a self-portrait.

The **bishop** wore magnificent robes while taking services or preaching sermons. This was originally done out of respect for God, but some bishops also basked in the glory of their own, and their cathedral's, power.

Priest

Bishop

Pope

The **bishop** also wore a pointed hat, known as a miter, and carried a tall staff known as a crozier. This was based on a shepherd's crook, and was meant to remind the bishop to care for ordinary people as a shepherd cares for his flock. The bishop's robes, miter and crook were often made out of rich, costly materials, and ornamented with gold, silver and jewels.

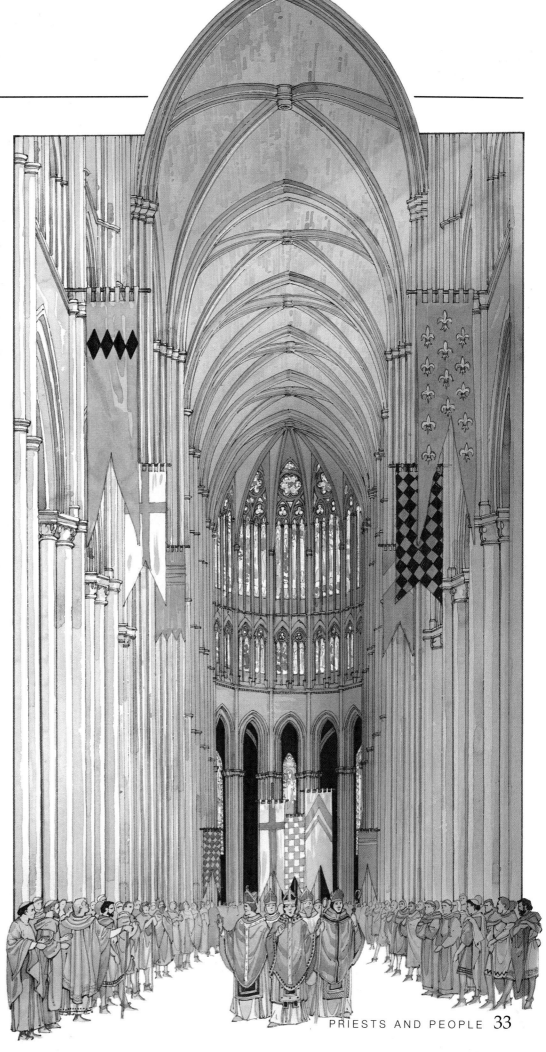

PILGRIMS

Men and women from all over medieval Europe traveled long distances on pilgrimage, to visit the tombs where saints or other holy people had been buried. Some pilgrims ventured further afield to the 'Holy Land' (the area around Jerusalem) where Jesus lived and died. People believed that time spent on religious journeys such as these would help win forgiveness for their sins and perhaps win them a place in heaven. Pilgrimages also provided the opportunity for an enjoyable, although sometimes rather dangerous, holiday in pleasant company. Special pilgrimage routes became established, with shops and hostels along the way. Bandits and highway robbers also seized rich pickings from pilgrims by ambushing them in wild and lonely country.

A French writer of the 12th century described a group of pilgrims setting out: 'The day was clear and calm. The girls and young men all recited poems or songs, and even the old people began to sing again. They all seemed joyful.... Even the little birds sang happily.... On the hillside...the cooks have set up tents.... There were many different wines, bread and pies, fruit and fish, birds, cakes and venison... plenty to buy for anyone who had money.'

Canterbury

Saint Chapelle

Winchester

Rheims

Chartres

Cologne

Notre Dame

Santiago

Toulouse

Cathedrals that housed the relics (remains) of popular saints could be sure of attracting many pilgrims. One of these was the Cathedral of St. James at Compostela in Spain. Beautiful, jeweled display cases, called reliquaries, were built to house saints' bones or other holy objects. Pilgrims offered money or goods to be allowed to see these, and paid extra to touch or even kiss them. They hoped that the saint's prayers would help them, and maybe even bring about a miraculous cure from some deadly disease.

Pilgrims' badges

St. Mark's, Venice

Pilgrim

J·E·J· MCMXCI

Old St. Peter's, Rome

To Jerusalem

On their journeys, pilgrims stayed at inns or hostels like this one from a 14th century drawing.

Some priests and preachers criticized pilgrims for enjoying themselves too much.

Pilgrims dressed sensibly for their travels. They carried clothing, food, money and a prayer book in a leather satchel known as a scrip.

Pilgrims traveling on foot carried long sticks to support them on rocky paths. They sometimes bought little badges, made of metal or cloth, in the towns near the saints' shrines, which they sewed onto their cloaks to prove that they had really been on pilgrimage.

MIRACLE PLAYS

Miracle plays – also known as 'passion' or 'mystery' plays – were another form of entertainment often associated with the great cathedrals. They consisted of scenes from the Bible, acted out at appropriate seasons of the Church's year, with dressing up, singing and dancing. These plays originated as parts of special festival services, with monks or priests performing all the parts. For example, in Winchester Cathedral in England, monks sang Easter choruses like these around 970:

'Alleluia, the Lord is risen today,
The strong lion is risen,
Christ, the son of God.
Thanks be to God, raise the joyful cry.'

Later in the Middle Ages, ordinary people took part in these plays, which they performed outside cathedrals. Some church leaders disapproved of this play acting. As the priest William of Wadington wrote around 1300 in a book called *The Manual of Sins*, 'Foolish clerks have devised another clear folly, which they call 'miracles'. Their faces are disguised by masks ...(and they) make foolish assemblies in city streets or in graveyards after meals, when fools are glad to come, even though they say it is done for a good purpose, do not on any account believe them that it is done for the honour of God, but rather in truth for that of the devil.'

J·E·J·MCMXCI

Some of the props and costumes used in the miracle plays performed in 1565 are described below: 'A griffon [a dragon-like monster]; a rib bone, coloured red; 2 coats and 2 pairs of dyed hose [tights] for Eve; a dyed coat and hose for Adam; a mask and wig for God the Father; 2 wigs for Adam and Eve.'

Although actors often worked for free, they sometimes received good wages for taking part in the miracle plays, as this record of payments made in Yorkshire, England, in 1483 shows: 'To the minstrels, 6d; To Noah and his wife, 1s 6d; To Robert Brown playing God, 6d.'

Throughout Europe church festivals were sometimes celebrated by processions as well as by miracle plays. The Procession of the Holy Blood was a Belgian celebration, while in Spain worshippers celebrated the feast of Corpus Christi and the French celebrated the festival of Saintes Maries de la Mer with processions. Cathedral clergy carried tall crosses, candles and banners – often acting out events in the life of Jesus – while the choir followed, singing hymns. Ordinary people joined in the procession, or knelt by the roadside, waiting for the bishop to bless them.

MONASTERIES

When Bishops founded new cathedrals, they also had to arrange for a 'staff' of priests and other clergymen to run the building for them. (During the Middle Ages, it was not thought fitting for religious women to take part in public life in this way.) There were numerous tasks to be done: services to be held, processions and festivals to be organized, choirs to be trained, precious objects to be cared for and guarded.

Somebody had also to arrange for the cathedral to be kept clean and in good repair, for its estates to be well run and its property well managed. Most important, wise and sympathetic men had to be available in the

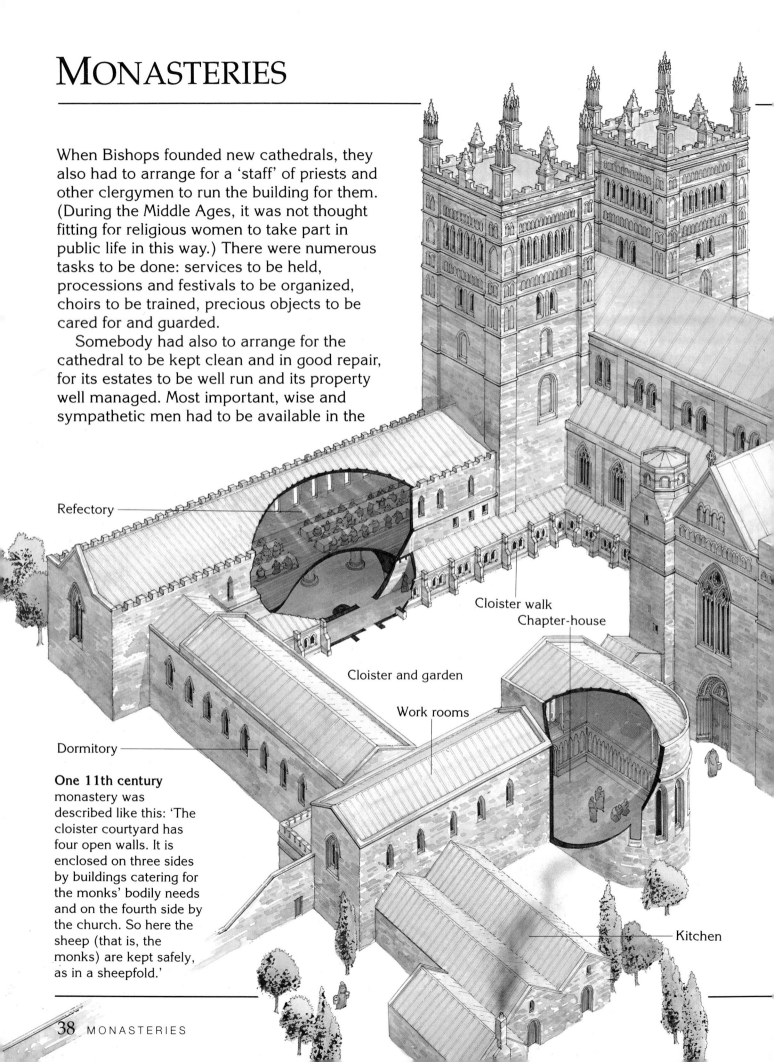

Refectory

Cloister walk

Chapter-house

Cloister and garden

Work rooms

Dormitory

Kitchen

One 11th century monastery was described like this: 'The cloister courtyard has four open walls. It is enclosed on three sides by buildings catering for the monks' bodily needs and on the fourth side by the church. So here the sheep (that is, the monks) are kept safely, as in a sheepfold.'

Transept

cathedral to offer spiritual help and guidance to visitors and worshippers.

Some cathedrals were run by a college of 'canons' – priests governed by a special set of rules. Other bishops preferred to establish a community of monks – men who had promised to live a quiet life of prayer and service to God – alongside their new cathedrals. The bishops had impressive buildings for the monks and their servants constructed beside their cathedrals, where the monks lived together, shut away from the outside world, concentrating their spiritual energies on the 'work of God.' Many of these cathedral monasteries survive today.

In the early Middle Ages, some parents offered their children to monasteries when they were only seven or eight years old, in the hope that they would become monks. This practice was forbidden around 1100, and, after that, men became monks because they wished to devote their lives to God and the Church. Their service could take several forms: they could become priests, church administrators, artists or architects, scholars or teachers. Some monks spent their lives looking after the welfare of people who lived in or around the monastery, or caring for the monastery buildings. Others supervised the monastery's lay-brothers and servants, and were responsible for running the farms and other property belonging to the monastery.

J·E·J·MCMXCI

Although monks lived in the monastery, they were not totally isolated. Many people came to visit and pray with them.

A DAY IN THE LIFE OF A MONK

1 am - 2 am In church for first services.

3 am Back to bed for a few more hours' sleep.

6 am Get up and wash. Prayers in church.

7 am Breakfast: bread, cheese, ale or cider.

7.30 am - 9 am At work in the monastery garden.

9 am Back in church for hymns and prayers.

10 am Main meal: fish, bread, eggs, vegetables.

10.30 am - 12 noon Clean buildings.

12 noon In church for midday services.

1 pm - 6 pm More work, writing or studying.

6 pm In church for evening service.

6.30 pm Supper (soup), followed by quiet rest and relaxation. Guests

often came to talk to the monks, or just to drink and play music.

8.00 pm Back in church again for the final service of the day.

8.30 pm Bed in dormitory shared with the other monks.

During the Middle Ages, many bishops began their careers as scholars, and invited other men of learning to visit their cathedrals to study or to preach. And many cathedrals supported a community of scholars in a monastery close by. According to the Rule of St. Benedict, which governed the lives of thousands of monks living in these cathedral monasteries, the monks' time should be divided between useful work and prayer. Often, this 'work' meant studying, writing, or teaching.

Some cathedral monasteries became great centers of book production, where monks copied out and illuminated beautiful Bibles and psalters used in cathedral services or for private prayers. Other monasteries were well known for their collections of important books on religious and learned topics. For example, Hereford Cathedral in England still has its magnificent medieval 'chained' library. The books are fastened to the walls with heavy iron chains, to stop them being taken away by thieves or by absent-minded scholars. Precautions like these were necessary, since all medieval books were valuable. Because they were written and bound entirely by hand, only a few copies were produced. A single volume could easily take hundreds of hours of hard work.

1

2   3

J·E·J· MCMXCI

1. **Plan** of a typical medieval monastery.
2. **A monk** painting from a manuscript. Many monks and nuns were great illustrators.
3. **An elaborate** manuscript illustration.
4. **Wealthy parents** sent their children to be educated by monks and nuns; boys went to monasteries, girls to nunneries. The monks taught children how to read and write in Latin.

4

PAST AND PRESENT

Although we usually think of the Middle Ages as the great age of cathedral building, bishops and their congregations have continued to plan and raise funds for the construction of magnificent cathedrals right up to the present day. Older cathedrals have also been completed, enlarged or sometimes – like York Minster or Coventry Cathedral, both in England – carefully repaired or completely rebuilt after damage in war or as a result of natural disasters.

Why do people continue to build cathedrals? What makes men and women today devote their lives to such enormous and time-consuming projects? Usually, their reasons are similar to those of the medieval bishops and their patrons: they are building to give glory to God and to draw attention to the Church's Christian message. No doubt they also welcome the opportunity to spend their lives creating something well made, strong and beautiful.

Liverpool Roman Catholic Cathedral in England. It was built between 1960-66, using modern materials like concrete and steel.

Rheims Cathedral in France. Building stopped in 1427, halfway up the cathedral towers.

St. Basil's Cathedral in Moscow, USSR, built in typical Russian style between 1555-60.

Cathedral of the Holy Family in Barcelona, Spain, built between 1883-1926.

Cologne Cathedral in Germany, a medieval cathedral with one spire added on last century.

Milan Cathedral in Italy, a striking white marble cathedral designed by a French architect and begun in 1386, but not finished until 1809 under the order of the French emperor Napoleon.

The 'Space Window' depicting astronauts, spaceships and stars (left), and a gargoyle portraying a workman (above), both from The National Cathedral, Washington DC, USA.

But most of all, at a time when the future looks uncertain and nothing seems built to last, modern cathedral builders are making a statement of faith. Like the architects and craftsmen who worked on the medieval cathedrals, they are building not just for the present, but for the years to come, and, perhaps, even for eternity.

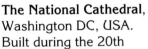

The National Cathedral, Washington DC, USA. Built during the 20th century in a medieval style using traditional building techniques.

The Cathedral of St. John the Divine in New York, USA (left). Work began in 1892, and the cathedral is still unfinished. Instead, money is spent to help poor and needy people in the diocese.

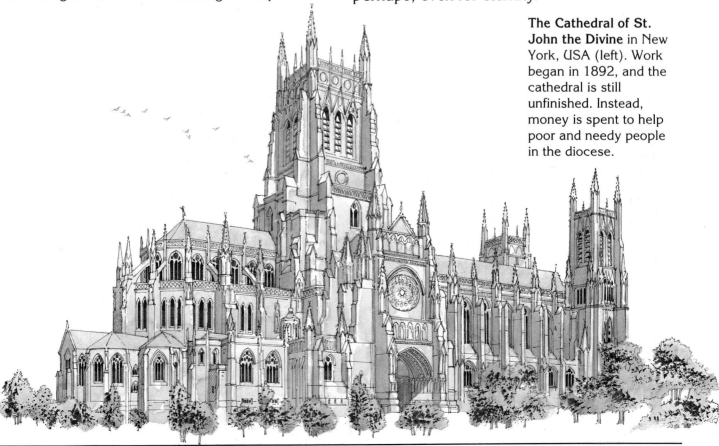

CATHEDRAL FACTS AND BUILDING STYLES

The bell tower of St. Mark's Cathedral in Venice stood for exactly a thousand years. The foundations were laid in 902, and the tower collapsed suddenly in 1902.

Cathedrals staffed by monks were famous for their charitable giving during the Middle Ages. For example, at Norwich Cathedral in England the almoner – a monk with special responsibility for helping poor and sick people – gave out over 10,000 loaves of bread each year. The monastic kitchens at Norwich also used 10,000 eggs a week. Even though medieval eggs are supposed to have been much smaller than today's eggs, it is still a surprisingly large number of eggs to get through each week!

In 1239, the tower at Lincoln Cathedral in England crashed down during a service. Three people were killed and many others were injured. So it is not surprising that one prayer said at Lincoln Cathedral contained the words: 'Deare Lord, support our roof this night, that it may in no wise fall upon us and styfle [suffocate] us, Amen.'

Enormous quantities of materials were used to build the great medieval cathedrals. For example, just one tower – the 'lantern' of Ely Cathedral in England – contains over 400 tons of wood and lead.

Cathedrals are very expensive to build. To help raise funds for rebuilding St. Peter's in Rome in 1507, Pope Urban proclaimed an indulgence – pardon for all their sins – to people who gave money to the cathedral-building funds.

The 13th century was a great age of cathedral building: 1220 saw building work begin on no fewer than three cathedrals – Amiens in France, Salisbury in England, and Brussels in Belgium.

The Dome of the Rock in Jerusalem is the only building in the world to have been sacred to three religions. It was founded as a Jewish temple, became a Christian cathedral, and is now a Muslim mosque.

There has been a church on the site of Cologne Cathedral in Germany ever since 873. The present cathedral dates from 1248. Its spire, however, was only added to the cathedral in the 19th century. The workmen followed designs that had been drawn up by medieval architects, and had survived, unharmed, for almost 400 years.

The cathedral of Santa Maria del Fiore in Florence, Italy, was probably the fastest cathedral ever to be built, completed in only 14 years between 1420 and 1433. While the great dome was being built, its architect Brunelleschi even had temporary restaurants and wine shops built up in the dome so that the masons would not have to make the tiring journey down and up again at lunchtime.

The first Russian cathedral was founded in 1050 – it is the Cathedral of Santa Sofia in Novgrod.

In Anglo-Saxon times, a monastic chronicler recorded a rather grisly list of relics that had been preserved in Canterbury Cathedral in England because of their holiness and supposed power. It began with the altar that was used every day for services, where 'the blessed (Bishop) Elphege had solemnly deposited the head of St. Swithin...and also many relics of other saints.' The list ended with the head '...of the blessed virgin Austroberta.'

St. Paul's Cathedral in London burned down and was rebuilt twice. The first fire was in 1087, the second in 1666.

Simple early cathedral

Old St. Peter's, Rome

St. Mark's, Venice

Santiago de Compostela

Toulouse

Styles of cathedral building changed over the centuries, from small, simple buildings to grand, towering constructions. On this page you can see some examples of cathedral architecture, and note how the shape, size and design of medieval cathedrals developed through the years.

The earliest cathedrals were simple structures, built out of local materials, either wood or stone. Often, a rounded apse was added to small, rectangular church to house the cathedra, or bishop's throne. Before long, wealthy cathedrals extended and expanded this arrangement, adding towers, porches, and extra buildings, as you can see in the drawing of Old St. Peter's in Rome, Italy. Building started here during the 4th century and the cathedral was added to several times in the centuries that followed.

Other early cathedrals were influenced by local styles of architecture. For example, St. Mark's in Venice, Italy, was built during the 9th century in a Byzantine style, copied from cathedrals and churches the architect had seen in eastern Mediterranean countries.

Romanesque cathedrals, like Santiago de Compostela in Spain, and Toulouse in the south of France (both built during the 11th century) also developed

Chartres

Notre Dame, Paris

Rheims

Canterbury

Cologne

the simple basic plan of early cathedrals, using massive pillars and heavy, rounded arches to give strength and solidity to their construction. At Santiago, tall towers were built at the west end to create an impressive entrance.

By the late 12th and early 13th centuries, cathedral architects began to experiment with new styles and techniques of cathedral building. In the earliest Gothic cathedrals, for example, at Chartres and at Notre Dame, Paris (both in France), the rounded arches and heavy pillars of the Romanesque style of architecture were replaced by taller, slender columns and pointed arches. Windows were larger, allowing space for brilliant stained glass, and roofs were higher.

This graceful new Gothic style was developed further in 13th century cathedrals, such as Rheims in France, which are remarkable for their light and elegant design. By the 14th and 15th centuries, Gothic architecture became amazingly complicated, daring and elaborate, as you can see in beautiful stonework decorating the famous late-medieval cathedrals at Canterbury in England, and at Cologne in Germany.

GLOSSARY

Aisle, extensions built on either side of a cathedral nave and running its whole length. ('Aisle' comes from the old French word for 'wing'.)

Almoner, a monk whose duties included giving money and food to poor and needy people.

Alms-giving, giving money to charity.

Altar, a table, usually made of stone, and covered with richly decorated cloth, where the Church service, known as Mass, was celebrated by bishops and priests. Cathedrals might have several altars, some in separate chapels dedicated to saints. The most important altar was called the high altar, and the most holy area of the cathedral was the space around the high altar.

Apse, semicircular area at the east end of a church or cathedral, usually behind the high altar.

Arcade, row of arches supported by pillars.

Ashlar, stone that has been carefully cut and shaped into neat, even blocks.

Buttress, a prop or support made of stone, designed to stop cathedral walls collapsing outwards under the weight of the roof.

Byzantine, a word used to describe people, objects or designs for art and architecture originating in the Byzantine Empire. In the Middle Ages, this powerful state ruled over an area including present-day Greece and Turkey, and the neighboring lands.

Cathedra, a Greek word meaning 'throne'. Cathedrals took their name from the fact that each of them contained a bishop's cathedra, or throne.

Choir, the area of the cathedral closest to the high altar. Cathedral clergy, including the bishop, stood in the choir during religious services.

Diocese, the area cared for and administered by a bishop.

Flying buttress, a narrow, graceful buttress shaped like an arch.

Foundation, a solid platform below ground, built to support the weight of a cathedral or any other building.

Galilee, a large, decorated porch built on to the west end of a cathedral. It was named after an area in the Holy Land where Jesus preached.

Gargoyles, spouts and drains used to direct rain water away from the cathedral walls. Gargoyles were often carved to represent monsters or people with strange or funny faces.

Holy Land, the area around the city of Jerusalem (which is in present-day Israel). Christians believe that it is holy because Jesus lived and died there.

Indulgence, forgiveness of sins granted by the Church in return for a payment of money. Usually, the money was given to a good cause, such as helping the poor or paying for a new cathedral building.

Journeyman, a fully trained craftsman who worked and was paid by the day.

Mortar, a mixture of sand, quicklime and water, used to 'sandwich' blocks of building stone together. Mortar sets hard as it dries, but crumbles over the years and sometimes needs replacing.

Nave, the main body of a church or cathedral, stretching westward from the choir. Ordinary people stood or knelt in the nave during cathedral services.

Oratory, a place where people say prayers.

Parchment, specially treated skins of sheep or goats, used to write on during the Middle Ages before paper became widely available.

Pigment, brightly colored powder made of earth, stone or chemical salts, mixed with size or glue to make medieval paint.

Pillar, a tall, straight column of wood or, more usually, of stone, used to support the cathedral roof.

Porch, a small building covering a doorway, and providing shelter for clergy and worshippers entering or leaving the cathedral.

Psalter, a book of psalms. Psalms are songs and poems in praise of God composed thousands of years ago by David, king of the Jews. They form part of the Bible, and can be found in the Old Testament.

Quicklime, a compound of the mineral calcium used in making mortar. It gives off heat when mixed with water, and rapidly sets hard.

Relics, the holy remains – often including bones, hair or clothes – of saints. Other relics revered by medieval cathedral visitors included fragments of the cross on which Jesus was crucified, and thorns from the crown of thorns he wore on the cross. Relics were not worshipped themselves, but were used to help people remember the Christian message and be inspired by the lives of the Christian saints.

Reliquaries, containers for relics, often made of gold and silver and decorated with precious stones.

Rib-vaulting, delicate stonework used to decorate the underside of a roof vault.

Roof bosses, clusters of carved stonework, usually circular in shape, used to decorate the points where the criss-cross ribs used in roof vaults met. Many roof bosses are beautifully decorated with carvings showing scenes from Bible stories, or bunches of leaves and flowers. Some portray magical and mysterious creatures as well.

Rose window, large circular window filled with brilliantly colored glass.

Spire, tall, pointed structure, built on top of a cathedral tower, often topped by a weather vane or a cross.

Templates, patterns for carvings in wood or stone.

Tie beams, thick, strong wooden beams, forming part of a cathedral roof. They were called tie beams because they stretched across the roof space, and held together the timber framework of the roof.

Tracery, a pattern of interlacing lines.

Transept, extension to a cathedral (or a church), usually built at the point where the nave joined the choir. The ground plans of churches and cathedrals with transepts are cross-shaped.

Vault, the arched underside of the roof. It could be covered with stone tracery (see rib vault, above), wooden planks or plaster. Often, cathedral roofs were decorated with paintings, carvings or gold and silver leaf.

INDEX

Note: page numbers in bold refer to illustrations.